REAL WORLD ECONOMICS™

How
Consumer Credit
and Debt Work

Laura La Bella

+6.73
+1.23
+21.64
+14.83 +9.19
+3.24
+32.47 +11.02
+2.35
.41 +25.06
+0.21
+2.42
+5.53 +12.41

10

▲ DJI

ROSEN
PUBLISHING®
New York

Published in 2013 by The Rosen Publishing Group, Inc.
29 East 21st Street, New York, NY 10010

First Edition

Library of Congress Cataloging-in-Publication Data

La Bella, Laura.
How consumer credit and debt work/Laura La Bella.—1st ed.
    p. cm.—(Real world economics)
Includes bibliographical references and index.
ISBN 978-1-4488-6785-1
1. Consumer credit—Juvenile literature. 2. Credit ratings—Juvenile
literature. I. Title.
HG3755.L293 2013
332.7'43—dc23

2012001086

Manufactured in the United States of America

CPSIA Compliance Information: Batch #S12YA: For further information, contact Rosen Publishing, New York, New York, at
1-800-237-9932.

Contents

INTRODUCTION

Consumer credit plays a big role in our society. Everywhere you look—from bookstores and clothing shops, to car dealerships and the Internet—people use credit to make purchases. We use credit to pay for everything from food, clothing, and furniture, to cars and vacations. Gone are the days when consumers would save their money for a large purchase. Now, consumers don't have to wait since a loan, credit card, or other form of borrowing can get an item in their hands quickly.

There's a price to pay for that convenience, however. Getting what you want, when you want it, is creating massive amounts of consumer debt. While it's easy to buy on credit, it isn't easy, or fast, to pay off those balances.

John and Kathy Smith are both well-educated teachers who make roughly $98,000 a year. When John quit his job to go back to school for another degree, their dual income was cut in half. Instead of altering their spending habits and looking for ways to spend less, however, the Smiths dug themselves

4

into more than $100,000 of debt. They maxed out twelve credit cards and owed large sums of money on two car loans and their mortgage. Their credit card interest rates went up when they missed payments, and they were charged huge late fees. Just meeting the monthly minimum payments grew difficult. Sadly, the Smiths aren't alone.

Credit problems were once a rarity in the United States. Consumer credit cards first emerged in 1958, when Bank of America launched the nation's first general-purpose credit card. Americans had shied away from "paying on credit" during the Great Depression and the Second World War that followed because saving was paramount and often crucial to a family's economic survival. After one-and-a-half decades of depression and war, however, consumers were again ready to buy. People were increasingly tempted by new conveniences for their homes, like kitchen appliances, washing machines, and dryers. These high price items put a strain on the family budget.

The concept of credit grew more popular when people realized they could buy items they couldn't afford to pay for with cash. Instead they would "buy now, pay later."

The widespread adoption of credit cards helped America's post-war economy grow enormously. Manufacturers and retailers grew and prospered. As lifestyles changed and people wanted more things they couldn't afford, credit card use continued to grow, and many people quickly found themselves in debt.

For responsible consumers, credit cards can be a convenience, rather than a source of trouble and worry. If one can pay off his or her credit card balance month-to-month or limit the use of a credit card to emergency situations, credit cards can be a positive financial tool. But for a family like the Smiths, who have racked up thousands of dollars in debt, getting drawn into the credit card spiral means falling further and further behind as finance changes, late fees, rising interest rates, and larger minimum payments make it difficult to pay even just a portion of the monthly bill, let alone the entire debt that is owed.

Understanding consumer credit and debt is crucial to your financial future. Your credit history begins the moment your first credit card application is accepted or you take out a loan. For most teenagers, debt begins when they head off to college. By then, many students have taken out education loans and have at least one credit card. Understanding credit and debt, how they work, and ways to use credit wisely are the first steps toward ensuring the health of your finances, now and into the future.

Instead of saving for a purchase, people use credit cards to buy items immediately. Today, the ease of online shopping has added to the many ways in which credit cards are used—and the many ways in which people can overextend themselves by racking up a lot of credit card debt.

CHAPTER ONE

UNDERSTANDING CONSUMER CREDIT AND DEBT

Access to credit, in the form of loans, mortgages (home loans), and credit cards, is an important part of the U.S. economy and vital to its health and growth. The ability to buy on credit has also ensured a higher quality of life for the American people. Loans to help pay for cars, new houses, and improvements and additions to older homes were designed to allow families to buy "big-ticket" items that they wanted and needed with only a small down payment. How else could average consumers be able to afford a home and a car, and how long would they have to save to get them?

A Nation of Debtors

While consumer debt has risen at a steady rate since the end of World War II, it's only in the last twenty years that the amount of debt has grown dramatically, as has the proportion of the average family's debt load to its income. There are a number of reasons for such a surge in consumer debt. For some

8

Maintaining a strong credit score is essential when applying for car loans, student loans, and mortgages. The stronger your credit rating is, the lower your interest rate will be. This could save you hundreds, if not thousands, of dollars over the life of a loan.

Americans, health care and insurance costs have increased significantly, leading many to use credit to help pay for medical bills. In addition, interest rates have often reached historic lows from the 1990s, encouraging borrowing by making it much less expensive. Much of this borrowing has taken the form of mortgages, or home loans. Usually a mortgage is the largest debt a family will incur.

When consumers use credit irresponsibly, trouble begins and can quickly spiral out of control. The more debt you rack up in loans and on credit cards, the harder it is to manage balances, due dates, payment amounts, and interest rates. Just one mistake—a late payment, for example—can begin a downward spiral of added late fees, over-limit fees, a crashing credit score, and higher interest rates. These added costs and fees will make it that much harder to pay back what you owe and dig yourself out from under the pile of debt that you've created.

The latest statistics surrounding consumer credit and debt are startling:

- The total amount of consumer debt in the United States is nearly $2.4 trillion.

- Thirty-three percent of that debt is revolving debt (credit cards), while the other 67 percent is from loans (car loans, student loans, mortgages).

- One in ten consumers has more than ten credit cards.

- The average household carries $6,500 of debt.

- Four-and-a-half percent of credit card holders are late by sixty days or more in their payments, thereby incurring steep late fees and interest payments.

What Is Consumer Credit?

Consumer credit is the money that a lender, such as a bank, makes available to a borrower. It is offered to consumers on the premise that the money will be repaid either in payments made on a monthly basis or in full and sometimes with interest. There are three types of consumer credit: noninstallment credit, installment credit, and revolving credit.

When applying for a loan, your credit score is used to judge how responsible you will be in paying the bank back for the money you borrow. After you apply for a loan, a bank or other financial institution will look at the types and amount of debt you have before making a decision.

Noninstallment credit is when a buyer uses a good or service and pays for it later. This kind of credit enables consumers to take possession of property or use a service immediately and pay for it within a short time period, usually thirty days. Utility and phone bills are an example of noninstallment credit. You use gas and electricity in your home, or maybe you own a cell phone. These services require you to pay for the total amount of the service used when the bill arrives. The balance owed can differ each month based on your usage, but the total amount is always due in full by a particular date.

Understanding Credit Cards

Using credit cards can make transactions simple and quick. But have you ever wondered how credit cards work? A credit card sale begins when you make a purchase. The store sends an authorization request to your credit card company for the value of the merchandise you are buying. Your credit card company checks your card limit to make sure you have enough credit to cover the sale. If you have enough credit, your credit card company reduces your credit limit by the sale amount and sends the store an electronic confirmation that the purchase has been approved. This all happens in mere seconds at the cash register.

Later, behind the scenes, the store sends your credit card company a record of the sale transaction. In return, your credit card company sends the store the money for the merchandise you purchased and then adjusts your statement to reflect the sale. The next credit card statement you receive will then detail the items you purchased and display the new balance on your card. The balance shows you how much money, or debt, you owe the credit card company.

Installment credit is when a specified amount of money is lent to a consumer to make a large purchase. The amount is paid back in a fixed number of payments over time, and interest is charged. Car loans, store loans for furniture, and mortgages are examples of installment credit. With these types of credit, a specific amount of money is borrowed to purchase a couch, automobile, or home, and the consumer agrees to pay the amount back in a set number of payments over the course of a certain period of time. Each monthly payment amount is the same.

Revolving credit refers to credit cards. A lender extends credit to a consumer, with a limit that depends on the debtor's credit history and his or her expected ability to repay debt. When you open a credit card account, the issuer of the card reviews your finances and gives you a credit limit based on what it thinks you can handle. You can't spend above that limit or your card will be rejected at the checkout counter. Unlike installment credit, credit cards do not have a fixed number of payments. Your minimum payment will change based on how much credit you have used, how much of the outstanding debt you have paid down, and what your interest rate is.

With revolving credit, the consumer has some control over the availability of credit. The difference between your credit limit and your balance is called your available credit. You can continue to use your credit card if you pay off your entire bill each month or make the minimum payments. This helps ensure that you maintain available credit and do not "max out" the card (reach its spending limit).

For example, if you have a credit card with a limit of $800 and you purchase $750 worth of goods, your remaining available credit is $50. That amount can be used to make more purchases. If you pay down your $750 balance by $100, your available credit increases to $150. If you pay off your entire bill, you again have $800 of available credit.

What Is Consumer Debt?

Consumer debt is the amount owed from the purchase of goods using money that is borrowed. A creditor or lender makes money available to a borrower through a deferred repayment plan. In exchange for being allowed to borrow money, the lender gets back the money plus interest (a fee for borrowing the money).

In order to make credit available, creditors are allowed to charge interest. This is often referred to as a finance charge. This is how lenders make money. For example, if a lender gives you $10 worth of credit, it might expect to be repaid $11 within the next two months. The extra dollar is the interest charged for the loan. Interest can be simple or compounded. Simple interest is interest charged only on the principal amount borrowed. Compound interest is interest charged not only on the principal, but also on the interest accrued during the length of the loan. Simple interest charges are less than compound interest charges.

Not All Debt Is Equal

Not all debt is the same. In fact, some types of debt are considered good debt, meaning that the benefit the debt provides to the borrower far outweighs the costs and risks of borrowing. Others, however, are considered bad forms of debt.

The Advantages and Disadvantages of Credit Cards

ADVANTAGES:

- Give consumers increased purchasing power.
- Decrease the use of cash.
- Credit card usage creates a record of purchases.
- Faster and more convenient than writing checks.
- There is protection for cards that are lost or stolen.

DISADVANTAGES:

- Items will cost more (interest and fees) if credit balances are not paid off in full each month.
- Available credit means consumers can buy things they cannot afford.
- Credit cards can increase impulse spending and buyer's remorse.
- Can lead to serious debt problems.
- Can be stolen and used without your authorization.

- **Mortgages:** A mortgage is a good form of debt, as long as the amount of debt you borrow doesn't exceed your ability to pay it back over time. Ordinarily, a home appreciates, or grows, in value over time, making it a good investment.

- **Car Loans:** Even though automobiles depreciate, or lose value, as soon as they are purchased and driven off the lot, a car loan is still a beneficial form of debt. Because an automobile is often a necessity for getting to and from work and for making daily life more convenient and efficient, it is considered a beneficial debt to take on.

- **Student Loans:** Student loans are an investment in your future. Education is the key to getting a better job, building a career, making more money, and having a more secure future. The benefits of higher education far outweigh the costs of borrowing.

- **Credit Cards:** Buying on credit and racking up significant credit card debt is a form of bad credit. Clothes, music, video games, electronic devices, restaurant meals, and other luxuries you might buy do not gain value over time. The short-term benefit of these items does not exceed the costs of borrowing the money to make these types of purchases.

- **Personal Loans:** A personal loan is a type of loan in which the borrower receives a lump sum of money from a lender, usually a bank, and is free to do whatever he or she wants with it. Personal loans have been used to purchase boats, make home improvements, and pay off credit card debt. Personal loans can be either beneficial or detrimental, depending on

A personal loan can be used for any type of purchase, including home improvement projects such as a new roof, a new furnace, or upgrades to a kitchen or bathroom. A personal loan is different from a student loan, which is used only to fund educational expenses, or a mortgage, which is used to purchase a home.

what the money is used for. If one is using the loan to pay off debt, a personal loan may carry a lower interest rate. If it's used for home improvements that boost the value of your house, that is money well-borrowed and well-spent. If it's used to buy a luxury boat that immediately depreciates in value and is expensive to dock, maintain, and operate, that is money unwisely borrowed and spent.

LENDING AND CREDIT POLICIES

According to the Federal Reserve, the central bank of the United States, total consumer debt has topped $2.4 trillion in recent years. Of this total, about $796.5 billion is from revolving credit, and about $1.6 trillion is from nonrevolving credit.

Simply put, consumers are in debt because they want things they cannot pay for in cash, so they borrow the money instead of saving up for a desired item. As a result, banks have made more debt available to consumers. But there's a benefit in it for banks, too. Lenders—which can include banks, credit card companies, credit unions, and retail stores—make money off the interest they charge on the loan. As a result, lenders, particularly credit card companies, compete with each other to attract borrowers. Yet once a borrower has signed up for a particular lender's credit card, a long list of fine-print rules and regulations increases the cost of credit. In the past, some unsavory credit card company practices have included the following:

- Credit card issuers used to be able to raise your interest rate without warning you.

While online bill paying has made it easier to make payments to your credit cards or loans, you still need to be aware of due dates and the steep penalties for making a late payment.

- Payment deadlines could be as early as 9:00 AM the morning of your payment due date.

- Credit card issuers could send your bill just a few days before its due date, increasing the chance you would pay it late and incur a late fee.

- Some lenders purposely kept their credit limits low, but offered consumers more cards, increasing the risk that a borrower would overspend and become swamped by debt.

- Some lenders practiced double-cycle billing, which allowed them to charge interest on the previous two billing cycles. This penalized consumers who did not pay bills in full and carried balances month-to-month.

These practices were halted when the Credit Card Accountability Responsibility and Disclosure, or CARD, Act went into effect in 2010. The CARD Act created laws to ensure that consumers are treated fairly and credit card terms are easier to understand.

CHAPTER TWO

CREDIT SCORES AND REPORTS

Consumers can obtain credit from a number of sources. Credit cards are available from banks, credit card companies, and retail stores. Banks offer loans for mortgages, personal use, and the purchase of automobiles, boats, or other large items. Your eligibility for credit is based on your income and your credit score. Having an income ensures a lender that you have the capacity to pay back the loan. Your credit score is used to determine the predictability that you will pay back what you borrow in a timely manner.

There are several types of credit scores, but FICO is most popular. Short for Fair Isaac Corporation, your FICO score ranges from 300 to about 850. The higher the score, the better chances you have of earning lower interest rates on loans and credit. Your FICO score is determined by your payment history, the amount of debt currently owed, the length of your credit history, any new credit accounts that have been opened recently, your recent credit history, and the types of credit you have used. Credit bureaus keep track of credit scores, and lenders review these scores against other borrowers when deciding whether to extend credit to you and on what terms, including what interest rate.

Calculating Your Credit Score

Your credit score is based on your payment history, the length of your credit history, outstanding debt, the type of credit you have used, and your number of credit inquiries.

- **Payment History:** Thirty-five percent of your credit rating is based on whether you pay your bills on time, whether a collection agency is attempting to secure payment from you, and if you have any bankruptcies or foreclosures on your account.

- **Outstanding Debt:** Thirty percent of your score is based on your debt-to-credit ratio (or how much debt you have compared to how much remaining available credit) and the balance of a loan against the original amount of the loan. In other words, the older a loan is and if it is in good standing counts more than new loans where the bulk of the balance is still due.

- **Length of Credit History:** Old is good. Fifteen percent of your credit score is based on the age

Paying your bills on time is the single most important thing you can do to keep your credit rating strong. Responsible borrowers set aside a few days each month to review their bills, make payments, and check their account balances.

of your accounts. Older accounts are better than newer accounts, which is why you should be vary careful when deciding to close an account. Also, opening new credit cards right before seeking a loan for a car or mortgage can count against you.

- **Type of Credit:** Approximately 10 percent of your score is based on the types of credit that appear on your credit report. The ideal mix of credit is three to five credit cards, an installment loan, and a mortgage. Credit scores with a healthy mix of credit show that you are responsible with your finances.

- **Credit Inquiries:** Too many inquiries into your credit report can hurt your score. When you apply for credit cards and loans, whether you are approved for new credit or not, the lending agency must pull your credit report. If a large number of inquiries have been made into your credit rating, your credit score can drop. It's important to note that checking your own credit report does not count against you.

WHY YOUR CREDIT SCORE MATTERS

Your credit score might be the most important three-digit number in your financial life. A high number can save you tens of thousands of dollars over the course of a lifetime. A low number can cost you just as much and can wreak havoc on your finances.

Your credit score determines how much interest you'll be charged for a mortgage, loan, or credit card. Yet it can also play a role in your ability to qualify for a loan in the first place, rent an apartment, or even get a job. It affects how much you will pay on a number of things, from interest charges to insurance premiums. A higher credit score can get you a lower interest rate on a mortgage or car loan, and it can help you pay off debt faster. Building a strong credit score can save you a not-so-small fortune over the course of your financial life.

How much does your credit score affect your finances? Here is an example of two friends who began their credit histories in college, but took two very different paths down the credit highway. Beth and Jessica both obtained credit cards in

Credit Score Facts and Fictions

1. The more money you make, the better your credit score. Fiction: While an increase in income can positively affect your debt-to-income ratio, this alone will not raise your credit score by much because your score is based on a number of factors.
2. Credit bureaus make mistakes. Fact: Credit bureaus can make errors, which is why it's important to check your credit report once a year to catch any discrepancies or errors.
3. Using only cash will improve your credit score. Fiction: Since credit scores are based on your use of credit, it's important to use credit regularly, but wisely.
4. All credit reports and credit scores are the same. Fiction: There are three main credit bureaus. While each will have most of the same information about you, it will not all match, which can affect your score. Checking your report will help clarify any errors or mistakes in any or all of these reports.
5. I can dispute inaccurate information on my credit report. Fact: You can dispute any information on your credit report that is inaccurate. The credit bureau has thirty days to investigate your claim. If the inaccuracy is found to be valid, it will be removed from your credit report.

college. Beth made all her payments on time, made more than the minimum required payment, never maxed out her credit cards, and kept her card balances below 30 percent of her available credit limit. Jessica often paid her bill late, maxed out her cards, and even went over her credit limit on occasion. She opened more credit cards and ran up those balances, too. She also rarely made more than the minimum payment on any of her credit cards.

When both women were ready to buy their first homes, they each applied for a $150,000, thirty-year mortgage. Because of their credit histories, however, the details of their mortgages were very different. Because Beth was financially responsible

Being aware of and improving your credit score can save you significant money over the course of your life. Keeping track of your credit report—which you can review at www.experian.com for free once a year—can also alert you to identity theft or reporting errors.

with her credit, she was able to build a credit card score of 740, which qualified her for a mortgage with an interest rate of 4.0 percent. Beth's monthly mortgage payment was $716. Jessica, on the other hand, had a credit score of 630. This qualified her for a 7 percent interest rate on her mortgage for a house that was the same price as Beth's. However, Jessica's monthly payment was $998. For the thirty-year term of their mortgages, Jessica will pay $282 more a month than Beth. That's $3,384 more a year, $33,840 over the course of ten years, and $101,520 over the course of thirty years.

WHO'S KEEPING SCORE?

Your credit score helps lenders predict how well you will or won't pay your bills and loans. Your credit score is used for more than just qualifying for a mortgage, car loan, or credit card, however. While lenders are the group most closely associated with inquiries into your credit score and history, there are other groups that are showing increasing interest in your score and using it to determine your level of financial responsibility.

- **Insurers:** More than ever before, auto insurance companies are using your credit score to determine the rate you'll pay for car insurance. Drivers with top credit scores can pay up to 31 percent less on their premiums. Those with poor credit scores can pay as much as 143 percent more.

- **Landlords:** It has become common practice when renting an apartment for landlords to

Your credit score is becoming more and more important to your daily life and financial prospects. Today, your employer, landlord, car insurance company, or utility company can check your score to see if you are a responsible person to do business with.

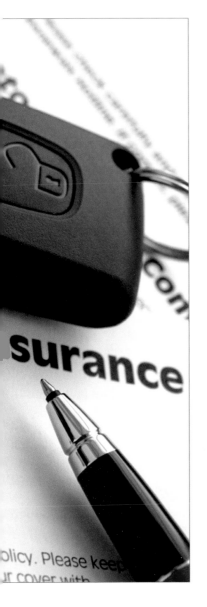

request your credit score as part of your application. If your credit rating is poor, you may be required to find someone to cosign your lease, or you could be asked to pay a higher rent or security deposit.

• **Employers:** According to the Society for Human Resource Management, more than 35 percent of employers now pull your credit report. Bad credit can be a sign of irresponsibility.

• **Cell Phone Carriers/ Utility Providers:** Cell phone service providers and utility companies, like gas and electric, may check your credit score before allowing you to sign up for a plan. If they see credit problems, you may not get the best cell phone rate or utility plan. You can even be turned down for service altogether.

CHAPTER THREE

WHAT'S GOOD ABOUT CONSUMER CREDIT AND DEBT

Consumer credit can have a powerful effect on the economy for both good and ill. An economic cycle is the natural fluctuation of the economy between periods of expansion (growth) and contraction (recession). Interest rates, employment levels, and consumer spending all determine the current stage of the economic cycle. When employment is high and people are spending, the economy is in a state of expansion (it's growing). When employment is low or when people lose their jobs, people tend to save more, look for bargains, and spend less. This can lead to a recession.

CREDIT FUELS THE ECONOMY

Consumer credit can help boost a nation's economy. In the Great Depression years of the 1930s, the stimulus program known as the New Deal gave Americans greater access to consumer credit. The New Deal was a series of economic programs implemented in the United States between 1933 and 1936 by

President Franklin D. Roosevelt. The programs were the president's response to the Great Depression and focused on the "3 R's": relief, recovery, and reform. These programs provided relief for the unemployed and the poor, fostered the recovery of the economy, and helped to reform the country's financial system to prevent another stock market crash and depression from occurring.

Providing greater access to consumer credit, especially during times of economic decline, can boost the economy. When credit is available and at lower interest rates, people spend more. When we buy something, the money we use to pay for a product doesn't stop at the store where the good or service

Consumer credit is important for maintaining a healthy economy. As people buy products, it creates demand, which means companies will continue to produce more products. This keeps workers employed and the economy strong.

was purchased. When people spend more, the demand for consumer goods increases, which creates more production of goods. More production means manufacturers are buying supplies and hiring workers to make enough goods to meet rising consumer

Making a big-ticket purchase, like a car, has a ripple effect on the economy. When you buy a car, the salesperson, dealership, manufacturer, supplier, and auto industry workers all make money and spend some of it in turn. Your one purchase begins a chain reaction that benefits people at all points within the industry and throughout the wider economy.

demand. More money is circulating through the economy, and when spending increases throughout the economy, earnings often do also. Increased earnings and incomes lead to still more consumer demand and spending, and a positive economic feedback cycle has begun.

Let's look at how buying a car impacts more than just the dealership where the car was purchased. When you buy a car, the salesperson often makes money off the sale, called a commission, and the dealership also makes money. The dealership then buys another car from the factory to replace the one you bought. The factory uses the money it received from the dealership to pay its workers' salaries and to buy parts from suppliers to keep making more cars. The supplier, in turn, makes money and pays its workers to produce the parts needed to build the car. Car industry employees who are getting steady paychecks are spending their money in other segments of the consumer economy, boosting demand and profits there. Overall, the economy expands and grows. This is how consumer spending drives the American economy.

Some consumer debt is actually healthy for the economy. It means

Types of Credit Cards

So many different types of credit cards exist, it's difficult to decide which one is best. Much of the decision making regarding the choice of a credit card should depend on how you intend to use it. Below is a summary of the most popular kinds of credit cards and how their benefits work.

- Balance transfer cards: These cards help you manage debt by allowing you to transfer a balance from a high-interest credit card to a low-interest card. This means that more of your monthly payment can go toward paying the principal of your balance and not the interest you've accrued.

- Rewards cards: These cards give you certain rewards in the form of cash back or points that can be used toward travel or other rewards items.

- Cash back cards: Cash back cards give you a small percentage back annually on the money you've spent using the card for purchases.

- Airline cards: Purchases made using these cards can earn you miles that can be redeemed for airline tickets to various destinations, hotel rooms, car rentals, and other travel-related items.

people are spending money, businesses are making money and hiring, demand is high, and manufacturing is humming. This is a healthy economic cycle. There is a delicate balance, however, to be maintained with consumer debt. Too much debt means people will spend extra money on paying down debt, instead of on goods and services. Paying down consumer debt is a good thing when getting one's personal finances in order, but it is bad for the larger economy. It is money that is diverted from the economy, money that no store or business receives and which does not trickle down to employees.

When consumer spending drops, the economy slows. Manufacturing decreases, workers are laid off, and many consumers begin spending even less, worsening the economic situation. A negative economic feedback cycle takes hold as decreased spending leads to lower business profits, higher unemployment, and further decreases in consumer spending.

MONEY MULTIPLIER THEORY

There is an economic theory called the money multiplier theory. This theory states that borrowing money to purchase goods and services transfers wealth to others, which boosts the economy. The example above, of how the sale of a car impacts more than just the salesperson and the dealership, is an example of the money multiplier theory. Wealth is spread to more than one entity.

This theory is often cited to justify increased government spending or tax cuts to stimulate the economy. When consumers have money available to them, they often spend it. This helps not only the national economy, but the economies of other countries around the world as well. The United States imports a large number of foreign goods desired by American

As chairman of the U.S. Federal Reserve, Ben Bernanke discusses the central bank's current monetary policy and changes to the interest rate. The Federal Reserve has the power to raise or lower interest rates and thereby directly affect consumer spending habits.

consumers. As American consumers buy more products, including imported items, the global economy expands and other nations can afford to buy American goods and services, thereby boosting the domestic economy and spurring still more consumer spending and global trade.

Stimulating a Sluggish Economy with Low Interest Rates

When the government is trying to jump-start a sluggish economy, one of the many tools it can use is the lowering of interest rates. Low interest rates make borrowing money less expensive for consumers, and that means more money flows into and through the economy. Most consumers are more concerned with how big their monthly loan or credit card payments are, not how much they are borrowing as a whole. Lower interest rates mean monthly payments are lower and consumers can more easily handle a larger debt load. This, in turn, makes them feel as though they can spend more money.

MYTHS and FACTS

MYTH The less credit I have, the better my credit score will be.

FACT This sounds plausible, but it's actually false. Two of the elements that make up your credit score are credit history and the types of credit you have. Having very little or no credit is just as bad as having poor credit. The best way to build a strong credit score is to have a consistent payment history and a healthy mix of credit, including credit cards, mortgages, and installment loans.

MYTH If I pay my bills on time and in full each month, I'll have a perfect credit rating.

FACT Paying your bills on time is only one of five criteria affecting your credit score. Even if you pay off balances in full every month, racking up high balances on credit cards can hurt your credit rating. Credit bureaus like to see responsible use of credit. They look at your debt-to-income ratio, and, if the ratio is poor (in other words, you have a lot of debt and not much available remaining credit), it will negatively affect your credit score.

MYTH Once a delinquent loan or credit card balance is paid off, the negative item is removed from your credit report.

FACT Negative information, such as late fees, collection accounts, and bankruptcies, stays on your credit report for up to seven years. Paying off a delinquent account won't remove it from your report; however, your report will indicate that the debt has been paid and the delinquency is resolved.

CHAPTER FOUR

WHAT'S BAD ABOUT CONSUMER CREDIT AND DEBT

A s much as consumer credit can help boost an economy, consumer debt—and the reduced spending it engenders— can cause an already ailing economy to slow even further. Approximately 70 percent of our gross domestic product (GDP) comes from consumer spending. The GDP is a measure of the value of all goods and services produced within a country in a given time period, usually a year.

CREDIT, SPENDING, AND THE GDP

A significant change in the GDP, whether up or down, usually has a major effect on the economy. The GDP is a measure of economic production and growth. When the economy is good, unemployment is low, and salaries and wages increase. This means people are making more money and spending more money. This translates to increased demand for the products that people want to buy and increased manufacturing and sales to meet that demand.

Brand-new Prius cars sit on the lot of a Toyota dealership. When the economy is weak, people have less money to spend on big-ticket items and luxury goods. Inventory of these items swells as buying and selling slow down.

When GDP is up, businesses make money because their products are in demand. When GDP is down, consumer spending decreases, and the demand for products falls. This translates into lower profits for businesses, employee layoffs, higher

unemployment, lower income and wages, and further reductions in consumer spending. A vicious downward economic cycle is underway.

When consumers spend less, products are not purchased as often or in as great a quantity. If you decide to wait on buying a car because you don't feel you have enough money and/or your debt load is already too high, the salesperson misses out on an opportunity to make a commission and the dealership loses profits. The automobile factory slows down its production of cars because fewer are being sold. The factory may even lay off workers because there isn't enough work to go around. Suppliers, who make the parts for the cars, also see a decline in orders from factories, so they let workers go. Across the board, spending dries up and money is drained from the economy. If a consumer cannot buy a car, it affects not only the consumer, but a whole line of other people and businesses, as cash stops circulating throughout the economy.

Bad Credit Card Habits That Lead to Debt Disaster

- **Charging purchases to a credit card instead of paying in cash:** If you have the money in hand, pay for purchases in cash. Small charges of $10 or $20 can add up quickly on your credit card, especially if you already have a large outstanding balance. If you can't pay off your card each month, you're now paying more interest because of all of these small but numerous charges.

- **Paying bills in no particular order:** If you have trouble paying your bills each month, prioritize what you need to pay first. Always pay for living expenses first. You need a roof over your head and a car to get to work.

- **Not checking your credit report:** Pulling and reviewing your credit report once a year can help you catch errors that will cause your credit rating to drop, which affects your ability to qualify for loans and better interest rates. It's free to request a copy of your credit report once a year from each of the three major credit bureaus.

- **Using a retail store credit card to take advantage of discounts:** Store credit cards carry some of the highest interest rates. If you can't pay off the balance each month, you'll end up paying more for a product, negating any discount you initially received.

- **Making late credit card payments:** One late fee of $35 doesn't sound like much, but you'll be amazed at how fast one missed payment can throw your account into default and triple your interest rate, causing you to owe even more money. With your payment history counting as much as 30 percent toward your credit score, that late payment stays on your credit report for a few years, negatively affecting your score. That's a high price to pay for one late fee.

THE PSYCHOLOGY OF CONSUMER CREDIT

The availability of credit influences how people spend money. A $10,000 family cruise to Alaska is easier to afford when you can pay for it over three years and not in one lump sum in advance. When you buy things on credit, expensive dinners, nice clothing, and extras like going to movies and concerts are easily available. When consumers must pay cash for purchases and operate within a fixed budget, they are faced with choices. It's dinner or a movie. It's one nice sweater or several lower-quality ones, rather than a season's worth of new clothes. When consumers pay for items with cash, and they actually see money being taken out of their wallet or bank account, it forces them to be more thoughtful and deliberate about what they buy and how much they spend.

With credit, there is a gap of time in the purchase process. We can buy what we want on credit today and pay for it

The availability of credit influences how people spend money. Thanks to credit, nice clothing and extras like going to movies and concerts are easily available. Credit allows you to pay off these purchases over a period of time, rather than right away and all at once.

sometime later. Consumers don't feel as bad when they charge a purchase as they do when they pay for it in cash. Credit allows consumers to delay worrying about where they will get the money to pay for something until the bill's due date arrives weeks later.

Consumers will spend more money when paying with credit cards than when they are spending cash. A recent study illustrated this fact. A selected group of people were given the chance to buy sold-out tickets to one of the biggest concerts of the year. Half of the members of the group were told that they had to buy the tickets using cash; the other half were told they had to use a credit card. The group that was forced to use credit cards offered twice as much money for tickets than the cash-only group.

This example shows that for many people there is a disconnect between spending and using credit cards. Consumers pay less attention to price when buying on credit because, psychologists believe, consumers don't see credit cards as real money. They feel good about their purchases when they spend using credit instead of feeling bad about the amount of money they have just spent on a purchase.

THE RISK OF CONSUMER DEBT

In recent years, when the economy has been booming, Americans have borrowed money at an alarming rate. They have used the borrowed money on everything from vacations, grocery shopping, and dinners out at fancy restaurants to funding home-improvement projects, holiday shopping, new cars, and new and second homes.

When the economy begins to slow down, however, other factors influence how we spend. Unemployment or salary freezes (or even salary cuts) mean consumers have less money each month to make even their minimum credit card payments.

Several people stand in line at the unemployment office, waiting to file paperwork. These men and women lost their jobs when the economy slowed due to the tightening of consumer credit.

So the debt load increases each month as the balance remains undiminished and interest and late fees begin piling up. When people become overwhelmed by their debt load, consumer spending tends to be cut drastically (which can have a devastating effect on the health of the larger economy):

• Consumers spend more of their monthly income on paying off debt and its interest.
• Consumers buy less.
• Consumers tend to begin paying in cash to avoid racking up more debt.
• Consumers tighten their budget and either reduce or eliminate the frequency of their credit card use.
• People stop taking out bank loans for large purchases like cars and homes.

CHAPTER FIVE

REGAINING CONTROL OVER YOUR CREDIT AND DEBT

Consumers don't get into debt overnight, so there's no quick fix for getting out of debt either. When consumer credit and debt take a turn for the worse, there are a number of things you can do to regain control over your finances and set things right. But first off, you have to recognize you have a problem and take an honest look at how you got so deeply in debt in the first place.

Are You Living Beyond Your Means?

"Living beyond your means" is a common phrase used to describe those who spend more than they make, a habit made far easier and more dangerous with the easy availability of credit cards and other forms of credit. How do you know when you're living beyond your means? Here are four ways to tell:

1. **Your credit score is below 600.** Lenders use credit scores to determine whether they'll extend

Being in debt may be a challenge, but there are ways to pay off what you owe and regain control of your expenses. Start now by spending less than you earn, paying off credit cards in full each month, and using credit cards only in emergency situations.

you a loan. A score below 600 tells them that you're a risk. A score this low means a consumer likely has made late payments, consistently used a high percentage of available credit, and possibly defaulted on a loan.

2. **You are saving very little.** Right before the credit crunch, the average rate of personal savings was -0.5%. This meant that people were actually spending more than their income and had depleted their savings to fund purchases and credit debt.

3. **Credit card balances are rising.** If you can handle paying only the minimum balance on your credit cards, you're likely struggling to get by. Smart credit card use means you should pay off each month what you charge on your cards. If you can't, or can't pay off the balance within a few months in emergency situations, then you have too much debt.

4. **Your bills are out of control.** It's easy to buy new living room furniture when the salesperson breaks down the price to a small monthly payment. After all, what's an extra $45 a month? Yet that monthly bill is only one among several monthly bills you must pay. These bills start to add up, and before too long you find yourself with more expenses than you have income with which to pay them.

MasterCard's inControl Credit Card Helps Consumers Control Their Debt

MasterCard has recently introduced a new credit card, called inControl. The card allows consumers to set spending limits and receive real-time information about their accounts. The card is a customized spending management tool that helps consumers establish a budget and manage when and where they spend money and what types of purchases are acceptable. The card also lets consumers receive alerts, via text or e-mail, to help them know when they are getting close to their spending limit and inform them of payment due dates. The card was designed to help consumers spend more wisely and stay on track with their budgets and payments.

CLIMBING OUT OF DEBT

First things first: to get a handle on your debt, you need to know exactly how bad the situation is before you can begin to organize a strategy and map a way out. The first thing you need to do is gather all of your financial statements in one place and begin a chart. Go through each statement and list all of your debts—from credit cards, loans, your mortgage, etc.—in one column. Next to each, write down the balance of each card or loan, and, in a third column, note the interest rate. In the fourth column, write down each debt's minimum monthly payment. This will give you a solid idea of where you stand on each of your debts and help you get organized to create a budget.

Start building a strong credit rating now by learning the smart way to use credit cards. Organize your bills and pay them in full and on time. Never exceed your available credit limit, and do not charge anything you cannot truly afford.

If you don't have a monthly budget yet, now is the time to start one. At the top of a chart, write down your monthly income. Next, take all of the monthly payment information you just gathered and add to it any other expenses you have. These could include groceries, rent (if you don't own a home and carry a mortgage as part of your debt), and any other bills, such as gas and electric, cable, your cell phone, gym membership, and so on.

A budget lets you see how much money you are spending and on what types of things. It can help you see problem areas, like if you spend too much money each month eating out, or where you can find extra cash by cutting back. The $20 a week you spend on coffee might be better used as an extra debt payment instead. Consumers who are serious about cutting back on their credit card debt know that it takes patience and some sacrifice to get it done.

Before you begin paying down debt at random, take the time to call your creditors to negotiate better interest rates. If you've been making your payments on time, call your credit card companies and ask if they can lower your interest rate.

Managing Debt

There are several important strategies that will help you regain control of your finances and begin reducing your debt load. They are:

- **Ditch the plastic and pay in cash:** If you use cash, you'll pay outright for your purchases and avoid getting even deeper into debt.

- **Pay more than the minimum payment:** While it isn't always easy to find extra money each month, paying even just $10 more than the minimum payment will help you begin to pay down your high credit card balances and reduce your interest charges. As you free up more money, add more to your minimum payment until your balance is paid off.

- **Pay smallest debts first:** It can be overwhelming to look at all of your debt and figure out where to begin. One smart move is to pay off the smallest card balance first. Not only will it help free up one extra payment per month, it will also give you a sense of accomplishment, motivating you to stay on track.

- **Focus on paying off high-interest cards:** On every card statement, whether it's a credit card, bank loan, or student loan, you will find the interest amount you are paying each month. By paying off the card with the highest interest rate first, you'll pay less interest over time, saving you some money.

- **Transfer balances to a low-interest card:** Rolling a high-interest balance to a low-interest card can help you make the most of each monthly payment. This strategy works well if you are highly organized. Some balance transfer cards have low introductory interest rate offers. If you don't pay

The more credit cards you own, the more debt you can accumulate. While it's smart to have a wide variety of debt (from credit cards and loans), you don't want to use too much of your available credit at any one time. Work to keep your use of credit below 30 percent of what's available to you.

off the balance in full by the end of the special offer period, however, your balance could be subject to an interest rate increase, making repaying the balance more expensive.

Boost Your Credit Score

Building a strong credit rating while you're young can possibly save you tens or even hundreds of thousands of dollars over your lifetime. Knowing how your score is tabulated can help you improve your score and boost your rating. Here are five ways to improve your credit score:

- **Pay your bills on time:** Thirty-five percent of your score depends on your payment history.

- **Don't max out your cards:** Thirty percent of your score is based on how much credit you owe lenders versus how much is available to you. This is called your credit utilization ratio. Strive to use no more than 30 percent of your available credit.

- **Start while you're young:** History is on your side when it comes to your credit score. Fifteen percent of your score is based on the average age of your accounts. So start using credit responsibly when you're young.

- **Don't open several new accounts all at once:** This tactic not only lowers the average age of your accounts, but it also indicates to lenders that you might go on a spending spree with all of the available credit you now have access to. New credit makes up 10 percent of your score.

THE LAST RESORT: THE PROS AND CONS OF DECLARING BANKRUPTCY

Bankruptcy is a legal financial option that eliminates all of a consumer's outstanding debt when he or she is no longer able to pay off loans and credit card debt. It's considered the last resort for those with severe debt problems because, while it provides immediate relief from overwhelming debt payments, the negative repercussions of filing for bankruptcy are long lasting and far reaching.

Pros	Cons
Filing for bankruptcy stops collection agencies from calling, and any foreclosures and repossessions are halted.	Filing for bankruptcy means you will lose all of your credit cards (unless you paid them off before filing).
Bankruptcy can help you sort out your finances and get you started on rebuilding your financial life.	A bankruptcy filing will remain on your credit report for ten years. As a result, it will be hard to acquire any kind of credit or loan, including a car loan or mortgage.
Bankruptcy can't erase your student loans, but it will prevent your lender from taking aggressive action toward collecting payment.	Bankruptcies are public information, which means your name will be published in the newspaper and public records.

CHAPTER SIX

THE GREAT RECESSION AND THE CONSUMER CREDIT CRISIS

When does consumer debt become excessive? Consumers are carrying too much debt if even the promise of low interest rates does not encourage them to throw caution to the wind and begin spending more once again. When payment delinquencies and bankruptcies become rampant, as was the case during the Great Recession of 2007–08 and its aftermath, lending and spending plummet. Everyone suffers throughout the economy, including banks, other lenders, investment markets, businesses, corporations, and manufacturers, not to mention the average consumer.

BEFORE THE STORM: A CREDIT SPREE

The Great Recession, also called the Global Recession, Global Financial Crisis, or Credit Crunch, is considered by many financial experts to be the worst financial crisis in the United States since the Great Depression of the 1930s. The Great Recession resulted in the collapse of large financial institutions,

The Great Recession resulted in the collapse of major financial institutions and government bailouts of banks. Lehman Brothers, a global financial services company, was forced to close its doors in 2008 after declaring bankruptcy.

the government bailout of banks and major corporations, a severe downturn in the stock market, and a steep decline in consumer wealth. The crisis led to a record number of housing foreclosures, prolonged unemployment, and a dramatic and protracted decline in consumer spending. A significant cause of the Great Recession was the historically low interest rates that encouraged consumer spending. Mortgage lending, in particular, had become so relaxed that millions of people took out loans on home purchases that they could not truly afford.

Low interest rates make money less expensive to borrow, encouraging consumers to spend more. In the early 2000s, the federal government sought to stimulate the economy after the September 11, 2001, terrorist attacks by lowering interest rates.

In the years leading up to the Great Recession, historically low interest rates encouraged consumers to take out mortgages on homes they could not truly afford. When the housing bubble burst and the economy slowed, many homeowners defaulted on their mortgages and lost their homes to foreclosure.

Following suit, financial institutions offered credit cards, loans, and mortgages to people with less-than-ideal credit ratings and those who were already in a considerable amount of debt. Banks took on a lot of risk with these customers, all in an attempt to boost the slowing economy.

The short-term result was positive: consumers did indeed spend more money, and the economy avoided slipping into a recession. People bought cars and homes and racked up credit card debt. This period lasted only a few short years. The long-term outcome proved disastrous when, later in the decade, the government raised interest rates, creating a credit crunch.

Great Recession Facts and Figures

- According to the U.S. Bureau of Labor Statistics, one-third of Americans were at risk of unemployment throughout the recession. The actual unemployment rate reached a high of just over 10 percent.
- Forty-eight percent of homeowners saw the value of their houses decrease.
- Eleven million homeowners faced foreclosure.
- The average monthly unemployment check was only $293.
- Sixty-two percent of Americans significantly reduced their spending.
- There were 6.9 million fewer jobs in the wake of the recession than there were at its beginning.
- Thirty-three percent of retirement-age workers were forced to delay retirement for financial reasons.

THE STORM BREAKS: THE CREDIT CRUNCH

A credit crunch is when the availability of loans and credit is sharply cut back due to an increase in the interest rate. The conditions for qualifying for a loan become stricter, making it harder to obtain credit. The end result is that money stops circulating throughout the economy, and cash dries up. During the credit crunch of the first decade of the twenty-first century, banks and credit card companies were suddenly no longer

61

lending as much money to consumers. The loans they were making came with very high interest rates and were offered only to people who had an outstanding credit rating and strong collateral (capital and other forms of wealth that could be used to guarantee the payback of a loan).

When the government increased the interest rate, it affected those mortgages that had a variable, rather than a fixed, interest rate. A variable interest rate mortgage means the interest can change over the life of the loan. When interest rates rise, the interest on the mortgage's balance also increases, and monthly payments rise. When interest rates are lowered, the interest owed on a mortgage's balance is reduced, and monthly payments decrease. With a fixed interest rate mortgage, the interest rate you will be charged is agreed upon when you sign the mortgage and never changes over the course of the loan, regardless of subsequent interest rate fluctuations elsewhere.

During the credit crunch, home mortgage payments increased, and consumers were forced to pay more for their homes, resulting in less of their money being available for other types of spending. Added to this was the debt most people had accumulated from car and personal loans and overuse of their credit cards. Suddenly the credit crunch became a widespread consumer credit crisis. In many cases, the interest rate increase raised monthly mortgage payments so much that homeowners could no longer afford to pay them, forcing banks and lenders to foreclose on the properties. People began to lose their homes.

The credit crunch drained money from the economy. People stopped spending, manufacturing slowed, businesses failed, and workers were laid off. During the Great Recession, the unemployment rate was the highest it had been since the Great Depression. More than one in ten American workers were left jobless, in many cases for years. With rampant unemployment, consumers were now faced with even less income to use to pay bills and get by. Consumer spending ground to a halt, leading to even less manufacturing and more job loss. The economy had entered a long and deep recessionary spiral.

THE AFTERMATH OF THE GREAT RECESSION

The Great Recession forced consumers to take a hard look at their financial behavior. As a result, many people began working diligently to get themselves out of debt and in a healthier financial state. Consumers began paying off debt, cutting their spending, and saving more money.

The Great Recession forced people to take a long look at their spending behavior and financial well-being. People began to save money again, pay down their debt, and make smarter decisions about purchases.

The aftermath of the recession, particularly the credit crisis, forced some people to stay in one place longer. Housing sales slowed, and people were no longer moving as often as they did in previous years. Recent college graduates were also being more careful about their career decisions. More and more young people stayed in their jobs longer, instead of job hopping and taking chances on risky and unproven new career opportunities.

For the first time in decades, Americans again began to save more of their income. While this was good for their personal financial health, the lack of spending slowed the recovery of the larger economy. Retail sales, orders of goods, manufacturing, and hiring all remained sluggish for several years after the official end of the Great Recession in 2008.

Ten Great Questions
to Ask a Financial Adviser

1. I have a lot of debt. Where do I start when it comes to making extra payments?

2. I just received some money for my birthday. Should I save it or use it to help pay down some debt?

3. What types of products or programs do you offer people with considerable debt?

4. What are some short-term and long-term changes that I need to make to help me get out of debt and stay out of debt?

5. Given how much I owe, how much I make, and how much I spend, how long will it take me to get out of debt?

6. Should I use a credit counselor?

7. Who offers the best debt counseling services?

8. Should I take out a personal loan to pay off my debt?

9. How can I ensure that if I pay off my debt, my bad habits won't get me in trouble again?

10. What are the pros and cons of filing for bankruptcy?

GLOSSARY

bankruptcy A legal filing that eliminates all of a consumer's outstanding debt when he or she is not able to pay off his or her loans and credit cards.

billing cycle The period between billings for products and services purchased by consumers; this period is often a month.

consumer An individual who buys products or services for personal use.

credit The extending of funds to a borrower, who agrees to repay the lender at a later date, often with interest.

debt An amount of money owed to a person or organization for funds borrowed.

default Failure to make required debt payments on a timely basis or to comply with other conditions of an obligation or agreement.

delinquent Failure to make a required debt payment on time.

Federal Reserve The central banking system of the United States.

finance charge A fee consumers incur for the use of credit.

fixed interest rate An interest rate that is set and will not change over the term of the loan.

foreclosure The legal process by which an owner's right to a property is terminated, usually because of default on the loan that allowed him or her to purchase the property.

gross domestic product (GDP) The total market value of all goods and services produced in a country in a given year; GDP is calculated by totaling consumer, investment, and government spending, plus the value of exports, minus the value of imports.

interest The fee charged by a lender to a borrower for the use of borrowed money.

mortgage A loan to finance the purchase of real estate.

recession A period of general economic decline.

repossession The taking back of property by a lender or seller from a borrower, usually because of default.

variable interest rate An interest rate that changes according to the interest rate index.

wages Compensation paid to someone for the work he or she does.

FOR MORE INFORMATION

Canadian Centre for Financial Literacy (CCFL)
1110 Finch Avenue West, Suite 406
North York, ON M3J 2T2
Canada
(416) 665-2828
Web site: http://www.theccfl.ca
The goal of the CCFL is to teach Canadians to make informed decisions about their money and the financial resources available to them.

Department of Finance Canada
140 O'Connor Street
Ottawa, ON K1A 0G5
Canada
(613) 992-1573
Web site: http://www.fin.gc.ca
Finance Canada develops policies and provides advice to the government with the goal of creating a healthy economy for all Canadians.

Federal Reserve Board
20th Street and Constitution Avenue NW
Washington, DC 20551
Web site: http://www.federalreserve.gov

The Federal Reserve, the central bank of the United States, provides the nation with a safe, flexible, and stable monetary and financial system. The Federal Reserve Board's kids' page features questions and answers about finances from a kid's perspective.

Jump$tart Coalition for Personal Financial Literacy
919 18th Street NW, Suite 300
Washington, DC 20006
(888) 45-EDUCATE [453-3822]
Web site: http://www.jumpstart.org
Jump$tart is a coalition of 150 national organizations that share an interest in advancing financial literacy among students in pre-kindergarten through college.

Junior Achievement
1 Education Way
Colorado Springs, CO 80906
(719) 540-8000
Web site: http://www.ja.org
Junior Achievement is the world's largest organization for educating students about financial literacy through hands-on programs.

The Mint
Northwestern Mutual
Communications Department
720 East Wisconsin Avenue
Milwaukee, WI 53202
Web site: http://www.themint.org
The Mint provides tools to help parents as well as educators

teach children to manage money wisely and develop good financial habits.

National Council on Economic Education (NCEE)
122 East 42nd Street, Suite 2600
New York, NY 10168
(212) 730-7007
Web site: http://www.councilforeducation.org
The National Council on Economic Education is a nationwide network that promotes economic literacy for students and their teachers.

National Economists Club
P.O. Box 19281
Washington, DC 20036
(703) 493-8824
Web site: http://www.national-economists.org
The National Economists Club is a nonprofit, nonpartisan organization with the goal of encouraging and sponsoring discussion and an exchange of ideas on economic trends and issues that are relevant to public policy.

National Endowment for Financial Education (NEFE)
1331 17th Street, Suite 1200
Denver, CO 80202
(303) 741-6333
Web site: http://www.nefe.org
The National Endowment for Financial Education is the only private, nonprofit, national foundation dedicated to improving the financial well-being of all Americans.

National Foundation for Credit Counseling (NFCC)
2000 M Street NW, Suite 505
Washington, DC 20036
(202) 677-4300
Web site: http://www.nfcc.org
The National Foundation for Credit Counseling promotes financially responsible behavior. The organization offers high-quality financial education and counseling services.

WEB SITES

Due to the changing nature of Internet links, Rosen Publishing has developed an online list of Web sites related to the subject of this book. This site is updated regularly. Please use this link to access the list:

http://www.rosenlinks.com/rwe/debt

FOR FURTHER READING

Bellenir, Karen. *Debt Information for Teens: Tips for a Successful Financial Life* (Teen Finance Series). Toronto, ON, Canada: Omnigraphics, Inc., 2011.

Bochner, Arthur, Rose Bochner, and Adriane G. Berg. *The New Totally Awesome Money Book for Kids, Revised and Updated Edition.* New York, NY: Newmarket Press, 2007.

Butler, Tamsen. *The Complete Guide to Personal Finance: For Teenagers.* Ocala, FL: Atlantic Publishing Group, 2010.

Byers, Ann. *First Credit Cards and Credit Smarts* (Get Smart with Your Money). New York, NY: Rosen Publishing Group, 2009.

Chatzky, Jean, and Erwin Haya. *Not Your Parents' Money Book: Making, Saving, and Spending Your Own Money.* New York, NY: Simon & Schuster Books for Young Readers, 2010.

Collins, Robyn, and Kimberly Burlseon Spinks. *Prepare to Be a Teen Millionaire.* Deerfield Beach, FL: HCI, 2008.

Fisanick, Christrina. *Debt* (Opposing Viewpoints). Farmington Hills, MI: Greenhaven Press, 2009.

Fradin, Dennis Brindell, and Judith Bloom Fradin. *Borrowing.* Tarrytown, NY: Marshall Cavendish, 2010.

Gorman, Tom. *The Complete Idiot's Guide to the Great Recession*. New York, NY: Penguin Group, 2010.

Hall, Alvin. *Show Me the Money: How to Make Cents of Economics*. New York, NY: DK, 2008.

Heinrichs, Ann. *The Great Recession* (Cornerstone of Freedom). San Francisco, CA: Children's Press, 2011.

Humbolt, Karin. *I Want to Be Rich!: Financial Planning for Teenagers*. Atlanta, GA: Reynolds Publishing Company, 2009.

Lynette, Rachel. *What to Do When Your Family Is in Debt*. New York, NY: PowerKids Press, 2010.

Minden, Cecilia. *Using Credit Wisely*. Ann Arbor, MI: Cherry Lakes Publishing, 2007.

Tardiff, Joseph. *Consumer Debt* (Current Controversies). Farmington Hills, MI: Greenhaven Press, 2010.

BIBLIOGRAPHY

Andriotis, Annamaria. "10 Things Credit-Card Companies Won't Say." SmartMoney.com, March 8, 2010. Retrieved November 2011 (http://www.smartmoney.com/spend/rip-offs/10-things-your-credit-card-company-wont-tell-you-18808/#articleTabs).

Bankrate.com. "10 Bad Habits That Lead to Debt Disaster." MSN.com, June 16, 2009. Retrieved November 2011 (http://articles.moneycentral.msn.com/SavingandDebt/ManageDebt/10BadHabitsThatLeadToDebtDisaster.aspx).

Bonner, William, and Addison Wiggin. *The New Empire of Debt*. Hoboken, NJ: John Wiley & Sons, 2009.

Burt, Erin. "Why Your Credit Score Matters." Kiplinger.com, February 22, 2007. Retrieved November 2011 (http://www.kiplinger.com/columns/starting/archive/2007/st0221.htm).

Business Insider. "9 Alarming U.S. Consumer Debt Statistics." May 23, 2011. Retrieved November 2011 (http://articles.businessinsider.com/2011-05-23/markets/30101275_1_consumer-debt-credit-cards-student-loans).

ConsumerAffairs.com. "Pros and Cons of Bankruptcy." Retrieved November 2011 (http://www.consumeraffairs.com/finance/bankruptcy_02.html).

Curtis, Glenn. "5 Signs You're Living Below Your Means." Investopedia.com, July 12, 2009. Retrieved November 2011 (http://www.investopedia.com/articles/pf/08/in-over-your-head.asp#axzz1eSoa9LdA).

Finley, Steven. *Consumer Credit Fundamentals.* New York, NY: Palgrave Macmillan, 2009.

Finley, Steven. *The Management of Consumer Credit: Theory and Practice.* New York, NY: Palgrave Macmillan, 2010.

Gross, Daniel. "The Death of the Credit Card Economy." *Slate*, August 30, 2008. Retrieved November 2011 (http://www.slate.com/articles/business/moneybox/2008/08/the_death_of_the_credit_card_economy.html).

Historians.org. "Does It Pay to Borrow?" Retrieved November 2011 (http://www.historians.org/projects/giroundtable/Borrow/Borrow3.htm).

Investopedia.com. "The Bright Side of the Credit Crisis." May 28, 2009. Retrieved November 2011 (http://www.investopedia.com/articles/economics/08/credit-crisis.asp#axzz1dzY8uFr3).

Kiplinger.com. "11 Credit Card Mistakes to Avoid." August 2011. Retrieved October 2011 (http://www.kiplinger.com/slideshow/credit-card-mistakes/13.html#top).

Kiviat, Barbara. "The Credit Crunch: Where Is It Happening?" *Time*, September 30, 2008. Retrieved November 2011 (http://www.time.com/time/business/article/0,8599,1845818,00.html).

Krugman, Paul. *The Return of Depression Economics.* New York, NY: W. W. Norton and Company, 2009.

Lazzaro, Joseph. "U.S. Consumer Credit Falls Again, Sending the Global Economy a Message." DailyFinance.com,

October 7, 2009. Retrieved November 2011 (http://www.dailyfinance.com/2009/10/07/u-s-consumer-credit-falls-again-sending-the-global-economy-a-m).

Markman, Art. "Spending and Credit Cards." *Psychology Today*, January 26, 2010. Retrieved November 2011 (http://www.psychologytoday.com/blog/ulterior-motives/201001/spending-and-credit-cards).

Marples, Gareth. "The History of Credit Cards—It All Started in the 18th Century." TheHistoryOf.net, September 11, 2008. Retrieved November 2011 (http://www.thehistoryof.net/history-of-credit-cards.html).

McBride, Carter. "What Are Three Types of Consumer Credit?" Chron.com. Retrieved November 2011 (http://smallbusiness.chron.com/three-types-consumer-credit-1886.html).

Money-Zine.com. "Risks of Rising Consumer Debt." 2007. Retrieved November 2011 (http://www.money-zine.com/Financial-Planning/Debt-Consolidation/Risks-of-Rising-Consumer-Debt).

Murphy, Ann-Marie. "10 Credit Score Facts and Fictions." Quizzle.com, April 27, 2010. Retrieved November 2011 (http://www.quizzle.com/blog/2010/04/10-credit-score-facts-and-fictions).

Riggs, Thomas, ed. *Everyday Finance: Economics, Personal Money Management, and Entrepreneurship*. Detroit, MI: Gale Group, 2008.

Ruben, Matthew. "Forgive Us Our Trespasses? The Rise of Consumer Debt in Modern America." CSA.com, February 2009. Retrieved November 2011 (http://www.csa.com/discoveryguides/debt/review2.php).

720CreditScore.com. "Credit Myths." Retrieved November 2011 (http://www.720creditscore.com/credit-resources/credit-myths/#m8).

720CreditScore.com. "What Makes Up Your Credit Score?" Retrieved November 2011 (http://www.720creditscore.com/credit-strategies/what-makes-up-a-credit-score).

Thomas, Lloyd B. *The Financial Crisis and Federal Reserve Policy.* New York, NY: Palgrave Macmillan, 2011.

Wang, Jim. "50 Fun Facts About Credit Cards." Bargaineering.com. Retrieved November 2011 (http://www.bargaineering.com/articles/50-fun-facts-about-credit-cards.html).

Wiggin, Addison, and Kate Incontrera. *I.O.U.S.A.: One Nation. Under Stress. In Debt.* Hoboken, NJ: John Wiley & Sons, 2008.

Wright, Robert E. *One Nation Under Debt: Hamilton, Jefferson, and the History of What We Owe.* New York, NY: McGraw-Hill, 2008.

INDEX

About the Author

Laura La Bella has written numerous books for teens on careers, social issues, and economics, including volumes devoted to globalization, taxation, and commodities trading. She lives with her husband and son in Rochester, New York.

Photo Credits

Cover (headline) © istockphoto.com/Lilli Day; cover (credit cards) © istockphoto.com/DNY59; p. 6 Wavebreakmedia, Ltd./Shutterstock; pp. 8, 21, 30, 39, 48, 58 Mario Tama/Getty Images; p. 9 Jon Riley/ Stone/Getty Images; pp. 10–11 © istockphoto.com/Igor Dimovski; pp. 16–17 Comstock/Thinkstock; p. 19 Tooga/Taxi/Getty Images; p. 23 Digital Vision/Thinkstock; p. 26 © NetPhotos/Alamy; pp. 28–29 © istockphoto.com/Brian Jackson; p. 31 Charles Gullung/Taxi/Getty Images; pp. 32–33 Adam Gault/OJO Images/Getty Images; pp. 36–37 Blooomberg/ Bloomberg via Getty Images; pp. 40–41 Justin Sullivan/ Getty Images; p. 44 Jose Luis Pelaez, Inc./Blend Images/Getty Images; pp. 46–47 Mark Ralston/APF/Getty Images; p. 49 Ryan McVay/ Photodisc/Thinkstock; p. 52 WilleeCole/Shutterstock; p. 55 Ilya Genkin/ Shutterstock; p. 59 © AP Images; p. 60 © istockphoto.com/Kirby Hamilton; p. 63 istockphoto.com/Thinkstock; cover and interior graphics © istockphoto.com/Andrey Prokhorov (front cover), © istockphoto.com/ Dean Turner (back cover and interior graphic), © istockphoto.com/Darja Tokranova (p. 38); © istockphoto.com/articular (p. 65); © istockphoto .com/studiovision (pp. 66, 68, 72, 74, 78); © www.istockphoto.com/Chen Fu Soh (multiple interior pages).

Designer: Nicole Russo; Photo Researcher: Marty Levick